Needle Crafts 6

STITCHERY

SEARCH PRESS
Tunbridge Wells

Fabrics

Any kind of fabric can be used for embroidery: decorative work does not have to be done on special fabric. Try using tweeds, woollen dress weights, hessian (burlap), curtain and upholstery materials.

Threads

Use as wide a variety of threads as you can find. Odd amounts of knitting wools are useful additions to your collection, both thick and fine, nylon and wool, lurex mixtures and heavily textured threads suitable for couching. Raffia, string, cords (used for macramé), threads unravelled from fabrics, crochet cottons and those used for machine sewing as well as embroidery threads of all types.

If a fine thread is liable to tangle and knot while in use, first draw it through a block of beeswax. This can be bought at all good haberdashery counters.

Needles

Use the correct needle for the material and thread with which you are working. The *crewel needle* (sizes 5-10) has a sharp point and a longish eye useful for stranded threads. For thicker threads you will need a larger, heavier type with a large eye, or a *tapestry needle* (no. 20) with a blunt point. Blunt-pointed needles are always used when working stitches on top of others where the thread does not pass through the fabric.

A *beading needle* is very long and thin with a tiny eye which will pass easily through the hole of the tiniest bead. Always use a double thread when attaching beads.

A *leather needle* has a very sharp, triangular bevelled point which cuts easily through leather.

Carpet, or *packing needles* are thick and heavy with very large eyes suitable for taking string and heavy cords.

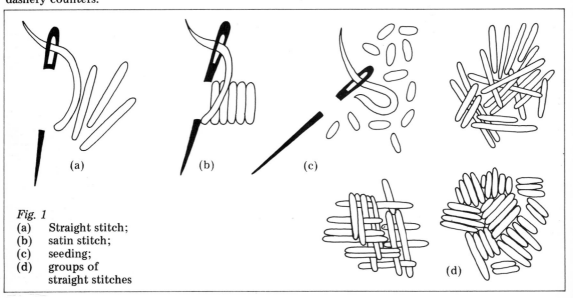

Fig. 1
(a)   Straight stitch;
(b)   satin stitch;
(c)   seeding;
(d)   groups of
        straight stitches

Preparation of fabric

Always place a piece of calico, medium-weight Vylene or firm cotton sheeting behind your embroidery fabric as a backing, and use the two layers as one piece. This gives a firmer hold to the stitches and provides a place to start and finish your threads.

Work a border of tacking stitches round the area to be embroidered and leave an allowance of at least two inches (5 cms.) extra fabric on all sides for making up.

Framing

Always work on a frame, however small your design. It will help to prevent puckering and will ensure an even tension.

To keep work clean

When you are not working on your embroidery, always cover it with clean tissue paper or a clean cloth fastened on with pins or tapes. An old pillow-case is ideal for this purpose.

Straight stitches

Above right: Straight stitches can also be used to express curves, as this example shows.

Below right: Satin stitch blocks may be used as a filling or to create heavy lines. They can also be scattered at random, as seen in Fig 1.

Page 4: Abstract on turquoise blue Dupion using padding over string, frayed fabric, chain and buttonhole stitch.

Page 5: Design based on an ancient candelabrum. The main branches are woven wheels over tiny pads of felt, with French knots and chain stitch.

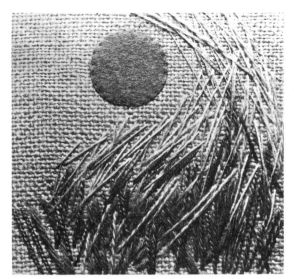

3

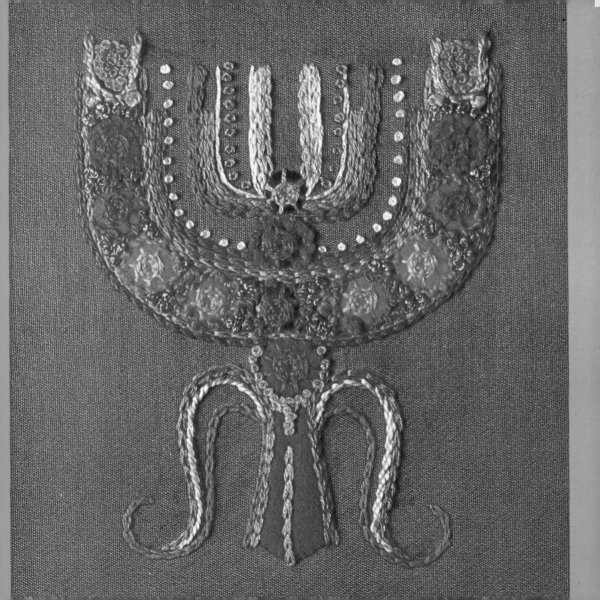

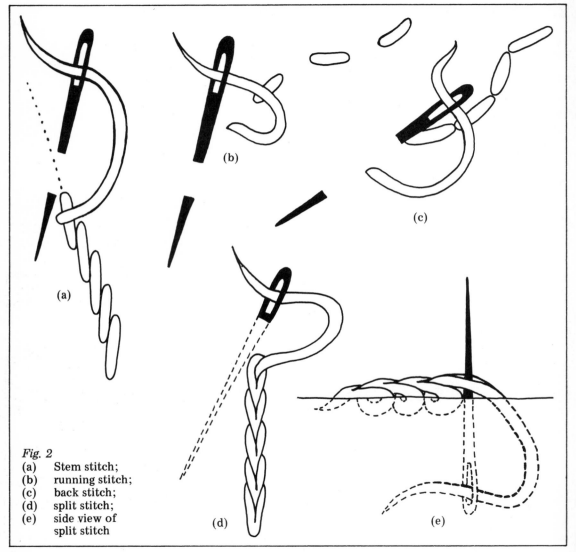

Fig. 2
(a) Stem stitch;
(b) running stitch;
(c) back stitch;
(d) split stitch;
(e) side view of split stitch

Stitches which make lines

Above left: Stem stitch and seeding.

Below left: Back stitch, split stitch and couching.

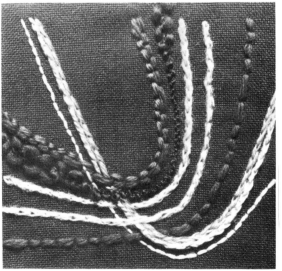

Fig. 3. (a) Whipped running stitch; (b) threaded running stitch using two colours; (c) Pekingese stitch

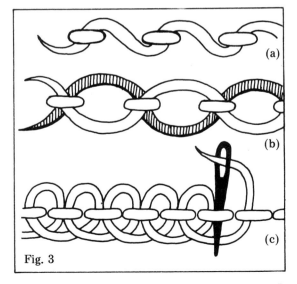

Fig. 3

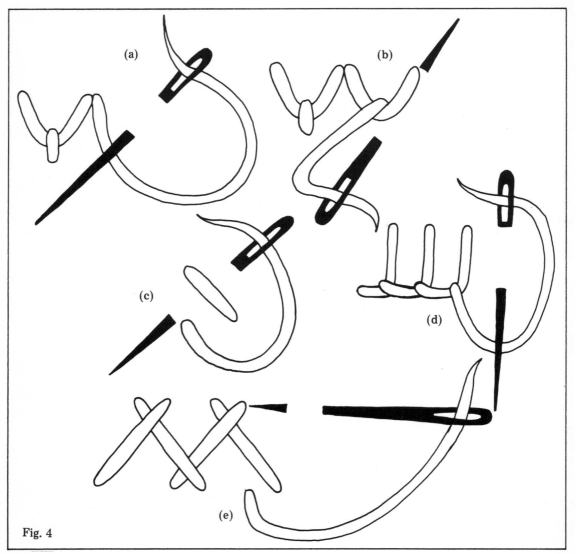

(a)

(b)

(c)

(d)

(e)

Fig. 4

8

Looping and crossing stitches

Right: Fly stitch worked in two directions, buttonhole stitch, interlocking and grouped. See also photograph top right on page 12.

Below: Cross stitch used as a filling and in groups. Herringbone stitch, and at the bottom, with another thread worked over it. More examples of herringbone stitch can be seen top left on page 12 and on page 13.

Fig. 4. (a, b) Fly stitch; (c) cross stitch; (d) buttonhole stitch; (e) herringbone stitch

Fig. 5. (a) Threaded herringbone; (b) tied herringbone

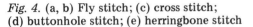

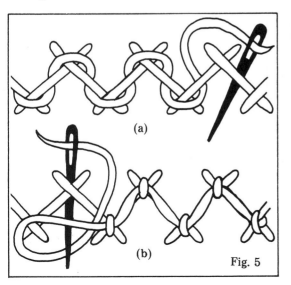

(a)

(b)   Fig. 5

Above left: Feather stitch open, double and closed; also Cretan stitch, another example of which can be seen bottom left on page 12.

Above right: Loop stitch *(top)* and Vandyke stitch *(below).*

Left: Feather stitch and Vandyke stitch used to suggest foliage. Note the use of different thicknesses of thread, including sewing cotton, and the varying width of the stitch.

Fig. 6. (a) Feather stitch; (b) Cretan stitch; (c) loop stitch; (d) Vandyke stitch; (i); (e) Vandyke stitch (ii)

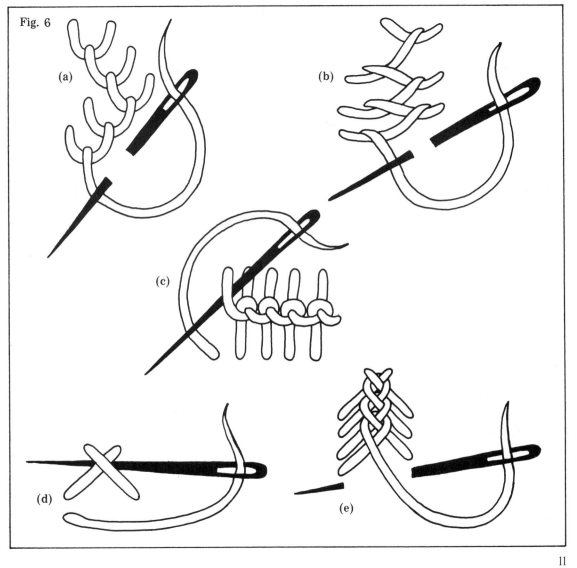

Fig. 6

(a)

(b)

(c)

(d)

(e)

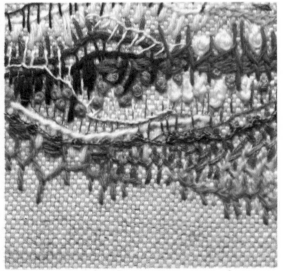

Above left: Herringbone stitch used freely; some worked over the top of others and some used to couch down furry, chenille-covered wire.

Above right: Fly stitch, buttonhole stitch and French knots. These versatile stitches take on a quite different appearance when worked unevenly in a variety of threads.

Left: Cretan, buttonhole and Portuguese knotted stem stitches, detached chains and French knots.

Page 13: Trees. The main trunk shapes are applied onto a printed cotton background, accentuated by Bokhara couching. The foliage is worked in herringbone stitch and couching.

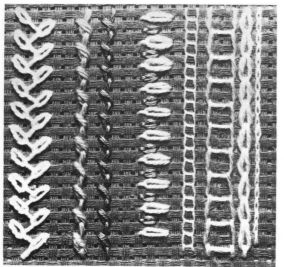

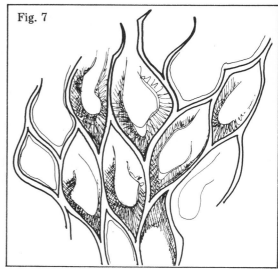

Fig. 7

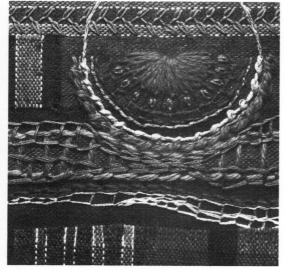

Chain stitches

Fig. 7. Pattern of lines on a fossil. Small areas of pattern like this may be interpreted in stitchery without any previous adaptation. Just choose which of the stitches shown here you will use and have fun creating a pattern.

Fig. 8. (a) Chain stitch; (b) open chain; (c) detached chain; (d) twisted chain; (e) feathered chain

Above left: Chained feather, twisted chain (similar to coral stitch), detached chain, open chain and chain (closed).

Below left: An example showing the use of all the stitches shown above. Notice how the open chain varies in width, closing and then opening again.

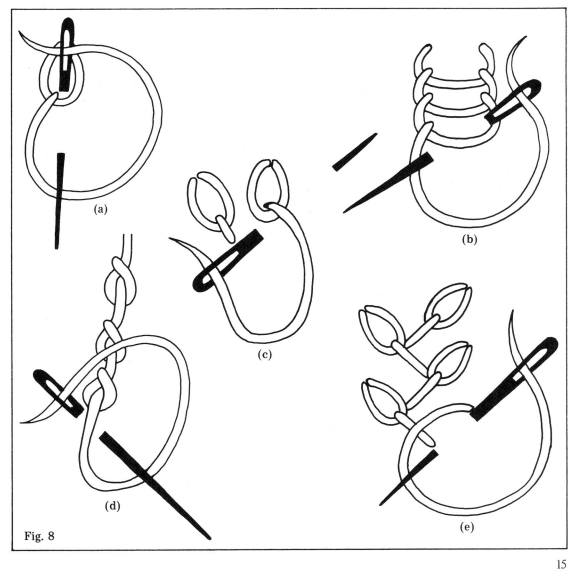

(a)

(b)

(c)

(d)

(e)

Fig. 8

15

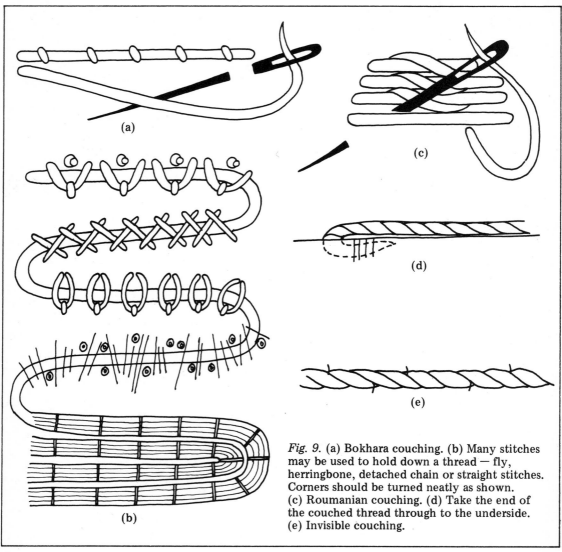

Fig. 9. (a) Bokhara couching. (b) Many stitches may be used to hold down a thread — fly, herringbone, detached chain or straight stitches. Corners should be turned neatly as shown. (c) Roumanian couching. (d) Take the end of the couched thread through to the underside. (e) Invisible couching.

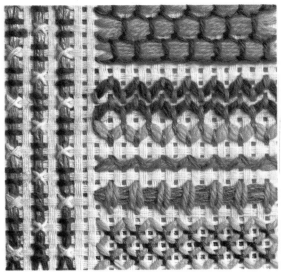

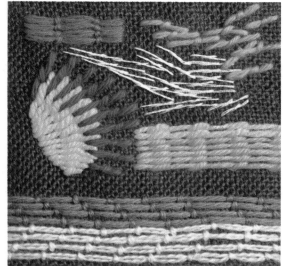

Couching

Above left: In this example threads have been couched down using decorative stitches to hold them, including buttonhole, cross, straight, detached chain and trellis *(bottom)*.

Above right: Bokhara and Roumanian couching are different from ordinary couching in that the same thread is used throughout, first laid and then held down.

Below right: Textured wools and heavier leather strips are couched because it is difficult to make stitches with them. Knotted string, buttonholed plastic circles and coils of thread are couched, some invisibly.

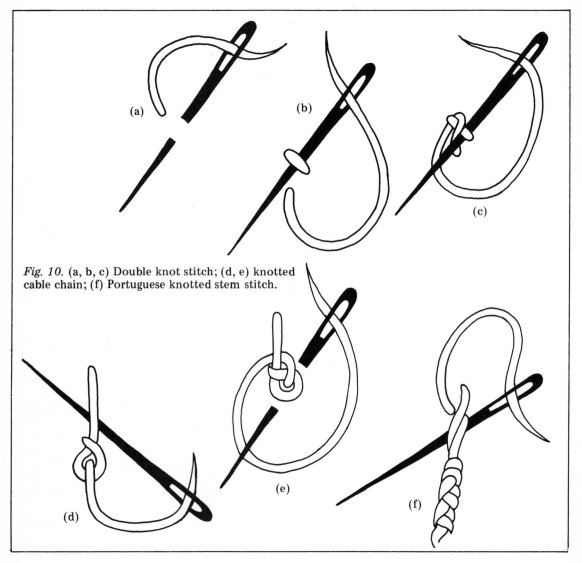

Fig. 10. (a, b, c) Double knot stitch; (d, e) knotted cable chain; (f) Portuguese knotted stem stitch.

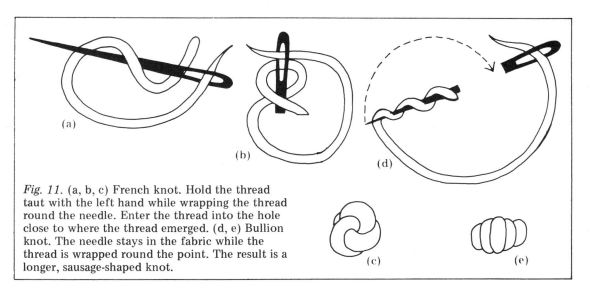

Fig. 11. (a, b, c) French knot. Hold the thread taut with the left hand while wrapping the thread round the needle. Enter the thread into the hole close to where the thread emerged. (d, e) Bullion knot. The needle stays in the fabric while the thread is wrapped round the point. The result is a longer, sausage-shaped knot.

Knot stitches

Below right: Double knot stitch, detached double knots, knotted cable chain, French knots, Portuguese knotted stem and bullion knots.

Page 20: Blue Landscape. Appliqué using silk on cotton. Buttonhole, buttonhole filling, herringbone, feather, fly, Cretan, Bokhara couching, straight stitches and sequins.

Page 21: Abstract design with padded areas, frayed fabric and appliqué. Raised chain band, detached chain stitch and square eyelets.

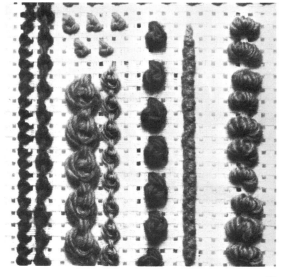

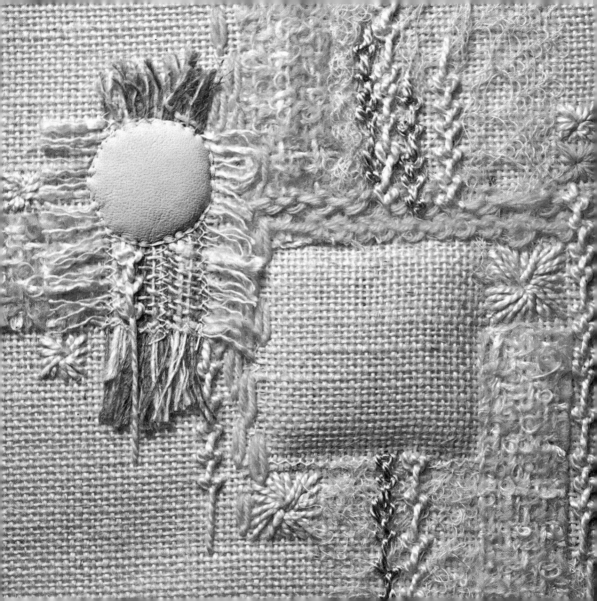

Building with stitches

Above left: Building patterns with stitches. Fly, cross, straight, buttonhole, chain, knotted cable chain, back, satin, whipped running *(below centre, left)*, and French knots. The use of different weights of thread makes these patterns more interesting.

Fig. 12. Try working a design based on buildings using some of the stitches to create patterns and textures. Ideas like this can be found on Christmas cards and in children's books.

Fig. 12

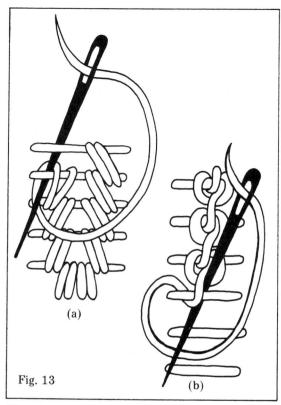

Fig. 13

Fig. 13. (a) Portuguese border stitch; (b) raised chain band.

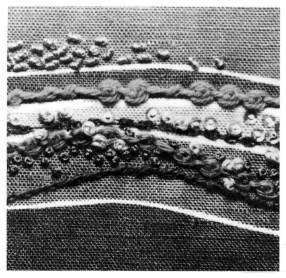

Above right: Raised chain band, Portuguese border stitch.

Below right: Knotted cable chain, twisted chain, French knots, bullion knots and sequins held down by French knots.

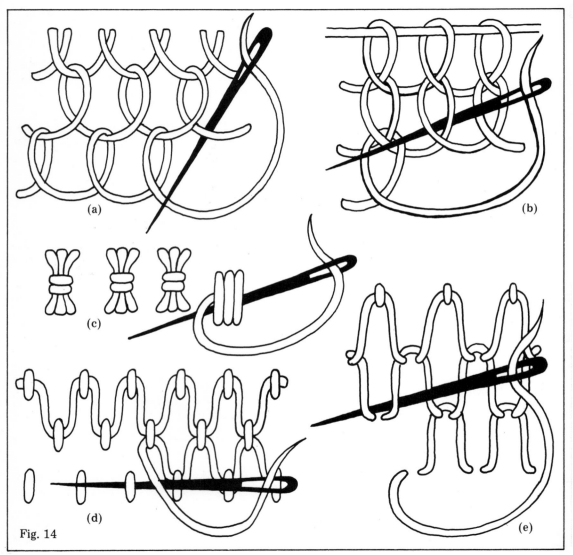

(a)

(b)

(c)

(d)

(e)

Fig. 14

Filling stitches

Above right: Buttonhole filling, Ceylon, sheaf filling, cloud filling and wave stitch.

Below right: A freely curving design showing some areas filled with sheaf filling, straight stitches, and Ceylon stitch. The lines are couched wool and string.

Fig. 14. (a) Buttonhole filling; (b) Ceylon stitch; (c) sheaf stitch; (d) cloud stitch; (e) wave filling stitch.

Fig. 15. Design based on a rock formation which could make use of the filling stitches seen on this page.

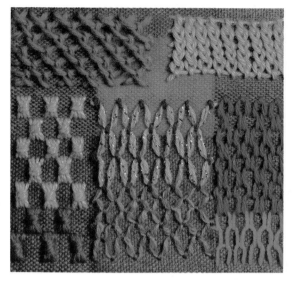

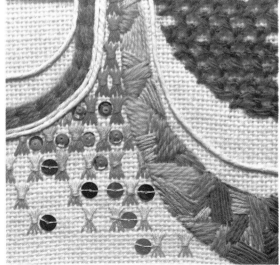

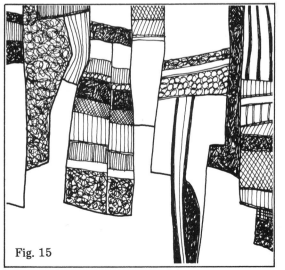

Fig. 15

Wheels

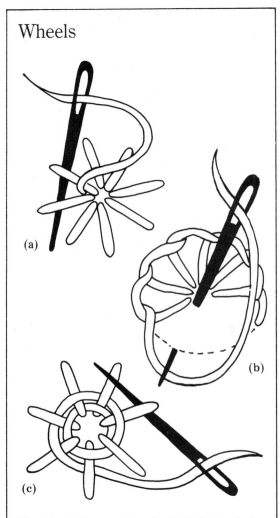

(a)

(b)

(c)

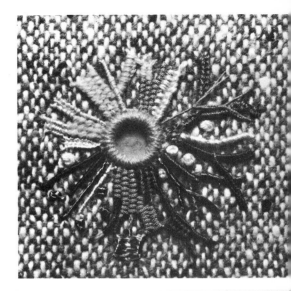

Fig. 16. (a) Stem stitch wheel; (b) buttonhole wheel; (c) woven wheel.

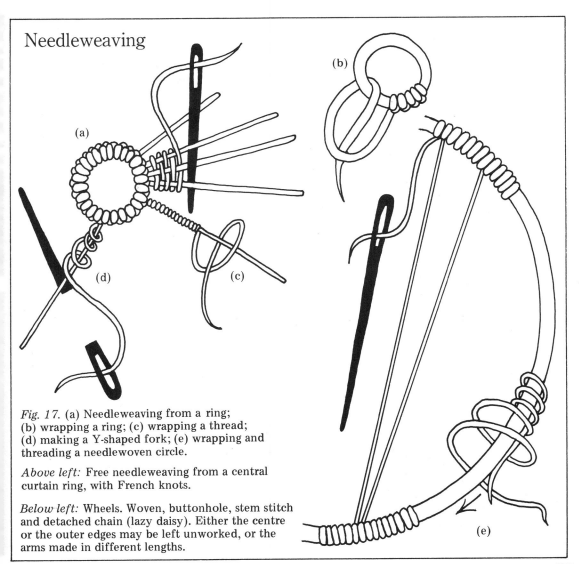

Needleweaving

Fig. 17. (a) Needleweaving from a ring;
(b) wrapping a ring; (c) wrapping a thread;
(d) making a Y-shaped fork; (e) wrapping and
threading a needlewoven circle.

Above left: Free needleweaving from a central
curtain ring, with French knots.

Below left: Wheels. Woven, buttonhole, stem stitch
and detached chain (lazy daisy). Either the centre
or the outer edges may be left unworked, or the
arms made in different lengths.

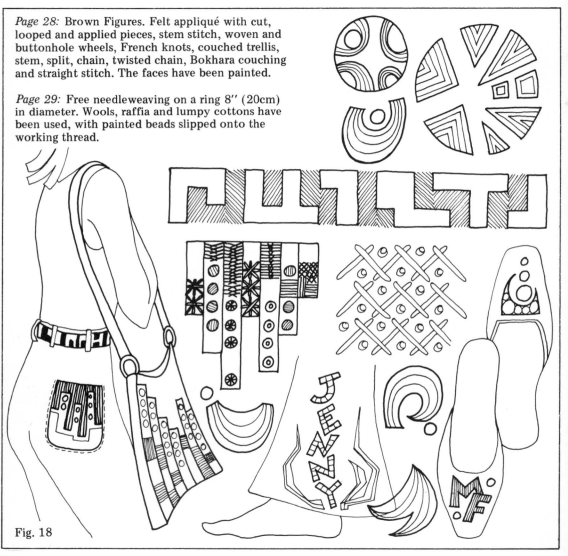

Page 28: Brown Figures. Felt appliqué with cut, looped and applied pieces, stem stitch, woven and buttonhole wheels, French knots, couched trellis, stem, split, chain, twisted chain, Bokhara couching and straight stitch. The faces have been painted.

Page 29: Free needleweaving on a ring 8″ (20cm) in diameter. Wools, raffia and lumpy cottons have been used, with painted beads slipped onto the working thread.

Fig. 18

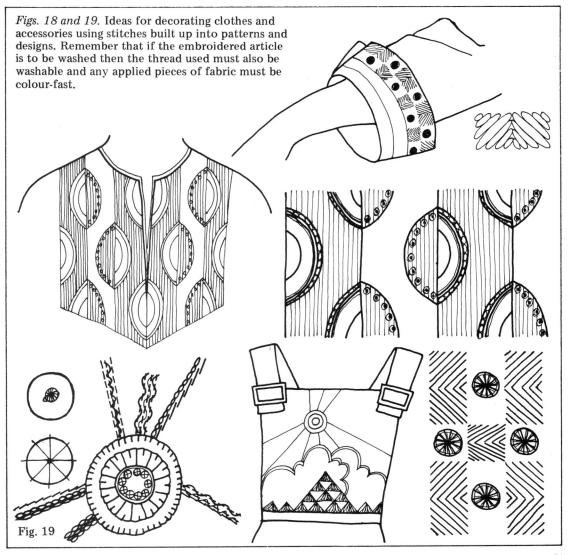

Figs. 18 and 19. Ideas for decorating clothes and accessories using stitches built up into patterns and designs. Remember that if the embroidered article is to be washed then the thread used must also be washable and any applied pieces of fabric must be colour-fast.

Fig. 19

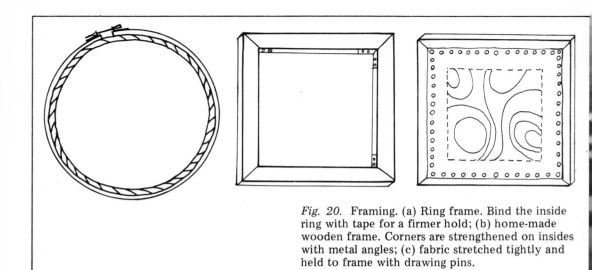

Fig. 20. Framing. (a) Ring frame. Bind the inside ring with tape for a firmer hold; (b) home-made wooden frame. Corners are strengthened on insides with metal angles; (c) fabric stretched tightly and held to frame with drawing pins.

Acknowledgments

Edited by Kit Pyman
Text and drawings by Jan Messent
Photographs by Search Press Studios

First published in Great Britain in 1979 by Search Press Limited, Wellwood, North Farm Road, Tunbridge Wells TN2 3DR.

Reprinted 1984, 1985 1987

Printed in Great Britain by Scotprint Ltd, Musselburgh

ISBN 0 85532 413 9

Front cover: Knotted cable chain, twisted chain, French knots, bullion knots and sequins held down by French knots.

Back cover: Flower Head. Wools, perlé cotton, stranded cotton and string using straight, sheaf and satin stitches and French knots on hessian.